Dining with the Dead

Fiona Sinclair

erbacce-press
Liverpool UK

erbacce-press publications Liverpool UK 2023

To find out more about Fiona Sinclair scan the QR code below

erbacce-press.com
ISBN: 978-1-912455-46-1

For my grandmother and Kim

Index:

Devil Dress	9
Stella	10
History Books	12
Chorus	14
High days	15
Writing Slope	16
Keloids	17
Best present ever	18
Mental Hack	20
Trust	21
Forgiveness	22
Undertaking	23
Closing the door	24
Calling Time	25
Happy go lucky	26
Missing Person	28
Monsters	29
More than one way	30
Ending	31
Time out	32
Ambush	33
Old School	34
Circus	36
Toy Run	37
'White Christmas'	38
Last Rites	39
Fear of letter boxes	40
Midwinter Monday	41
Letter	42
Why I don't write about refugees	44
Aging	45
Manly Hugs	46
Pillion	47
The decorators have left for good	48
Words fail	49
Clock	50
Still Human	51

Table	52
My father was	53
Dining amongst the dead	54
Bowing	55
Reflex	56
New	57
Sheffield Steel	58
Banning Barbie	60
Maxwell's silver hammer	61
Oakworth Station	62
Wonderland	63
Internet dating	64
Terms of endearment	65
Lucky Streak	66
Satan spends Sunday at a boot sale	67
The Quiet Room	68
Second Wind	69
Day Tripper	70
Family Portrait	71
When a sex symbol takes to sensible shoes	72
Synchronised Swimming	73
A game of hide and seek	74
Future conditional	75
Mr, Turner's dimmer switch	76
Ephemeral	77
Tattoo Tabular Rasa	78
Side Effects	79
Grief	80
Old enough to know better	82
Not as Young as they Feel	83
Card	84
About my mother's face	86
Single Bed	87
connoisseurs of comedy	88
Staying put	90
The Pleasures of Swearing	92
A Girl's Best Friend	94
It's my funeral-	96

Devil Dress

Demurely dependent on the hanger,
it might remain a wall flower in the wardrobe ,
but she knows the black jersey dress
has been designed by the Devil.
Gliding on over the body
it strokes breasts, brushes bum, smooths hips,
an augmented Eve skin,
winking with the promise of what lies beneath,
leaving everything to men's imaginations.
And after leggings and jeans,
its caress is an aphrodisiac,
so she sets off into the night
with an apple in her hand…

Stella

A gathering made glummer
by the assumption our colleague's life
was drab as this February day.
I thought her a nun in all but habit.
A strictly soap and water woman,
camouflaging her gender in neutrals.
As deputy head, she patrolled the school day,
with a nose for bad teaching and behaviour,
stealthily entering a classroom
abetted by soft soled shoes,
diminutive, she still discharged a glare that
winded gobby teenagers,
caused junior teachers to stutter.
In the staff room no lexicon for small talk,
only school business.
Her personality impenetrable as a safe
whose code very few could crack.
I imagined a life regulated by the school year,
last to leave the building and lesson planning
into the early hours, any free time devoted
to mass and confessing small fry sins.

But in the packed eulogy;
her qualification as a PE teacher

has the congregation raising eyebrows,
a nifty netballer herself,
took no sick note nonsense from pupils.
Lifelong Celtic supporter, sang in the stalls as a girl,
green and white scarf nailing her colours
to her study walls, every bit as the
gold cross and chain around her neck.
Still energy at the weekends
for Scottish dancing, first up at a Ceilidh,
capering her way to competition cups.
Greedy for off grid travel too,
leaving a footprint in every continent.
Since God the only man for her,
settling down meant a masters in English.
The glass ceiling as deputy head smarted but
became the woman behind the bungling headmaster.
In later life a serial committee member,
not rank and file but on the board
of local hospital and church council,
after meetings enjoying a good whiskey
with the parish priest.
We leave the church smiling at her hoodwinking us all.
Later, in the pub, 'dark horse, no idea, good for her,'
as we feast on the buffet
and her life rich as a Dundee cake.

History Books

Two hand me down books from mother,
Little Women and Alice in Wonderland.
As the covers shed and the binding perished,
I read the remains, filling in the lost pages verbatim.

A friend leant me Enid Blyton, but the Famous Five
made me a castaway in my 'only' childhood.
Christmas and Birthdays, relatives dismissed my appeals
for books with 'we don't know what you've read.'

No library membership. Perhaps a result of Nana
regarding borrowed books as 'riddled with germs,' so
baked them in the oven until their covers browned like
pastry, before she and her girls were allowed to read.

But I discovered second-hand book stalls at fetes.
With cadged half-crowns I bought Lorna Doone to dog
breeds, all stacked in the corner of my bedroom like
sandbags against a tide of holiday boredom.

And as my convent school prepared to mothball,
I would slip into the library with my school bag,
stuff with Dickens, Bronte, Hardy swag, that still
wink at me from my shelves when I scan for a book.

My tumbleweed twenties, I filled the days by chain
reading. Lord of the Rings sparked Gormenghast kindled
Dracula. Then the windfall of university at 32, spending
all day in bed, all day with Mr Rochester, Gatsby.

But teaching 'Streetcar 'for the tenth time, each lesson
became a stifled yawn and new texts were a chore.
Some teachers able to keep their appetites for reading
keen, but my free time, I crashed in front of trashy telly.

Retirement, I purged all texts books. Smiles at
reacquaintance with lost volumes. Treasure of unread
novels, Alan Bennett's 'The Common Reader 'getting
me freewheel reading, unfettered by lesson plans.

You arrive, and we set about making this a place where
you could comfortably park your slippers. Stalemate in
the sitting room. My books not dowry but dust traps,
shelved in Ikea efforts holding each other up like drunks.

Smarter cases are consigned to the lounge's far reaches,
mob visitors with minimalist rooms who think Kindles.
But I would sooner sacrifice my hoarded handbags,
because each book has more than one story to tell.

Chorus

It could even be heard in Sittingbourne,
a town that slept with one eye open.
And in the village, disturbed at dawn by a dream,
I would lie and pick out: karaoke sparrows,
black bird tenors, blue tit rockers.
In truth, less a chorus, more a vast warming up.
But any nightmares clinging to my waking mind
would be noise blasted back to where they belonged,
then suddenly silence, as if the day had rapped its baton.

In reality, not an ode to dawn, but a chest puffed chant,
staking claim over thickets for roosting, nesting rights.
But today, farmers are selling the family silver,
construction companies grub countryside,
planting acres of new builds with paved over drives
and low maintenance gardens.
So wild birds, like council tenants
in premium London boroughs, have been moved on.
Now, when I wake at dawn, a lone black bird sounds
the last post for the dawn chorus.

High days

Finally, our diaries align,
we take a trip to Charleston Farmhouse.
Parking up, a sudden down pour
plays percussion on the car roof.
We set about the picnic, silly with laughter.
An elaborate hopscotch, avoiding puddles,
to reach the house. Coo at Vanessa's gift for
upcycling functional furniture into art.
Outside, the sun has switched back on.
Squelching around the cottage garden
we exclaim at the craft behind chaotic borders.
The satnav decides to augment the day,
shuns the savage M25, takes us home
on the tamer A roads through the Weald.
Gushed 'We must do this again soon.'
I pan the internet for further treasure,
but dates refuse to conjugate where work
and family overwhelm and snatched free time
is shared with closer chums. No schoolgirl sulks,
rather an understanding that we are not in the first tier
of each other's friendships, but supernumerary,
meant for these high days whose antics are
still posted on our memories like indelible selfies.

Writing Slope

Daintiness suggests it was crafted
for a Victorian woman's life and person.
Gift from a husband or father no doubt.
Its tiny key meant for delicate hands, kept soft
by glove etiquette that swiftly dipped
pen nibs into the neat ink jars without
a dribble, to write in elegant copper plate.
Passed down by a series of 'careful owners',
the walnut box now placed into my hands,
big as a man's and garden weathered,
handwriting, a primary school scrawl.
I imagine a 150 years' worth of letters
that emails and texts have now killed off.
Instead, my poems are shaped over weeks,
on the slope that is better company than a laptop,
poems personal as letters, posted out
to whom it may concern.

Keloids

Bulimic scars that tell tales of a 'past '.
Grotesquely garlanding my face,
spreading like a botched tattoo
across my shoulders. Hidden under
sleeves to avoid bold 'What are those?'
Second crop in my 40s courtesy of menopause,
apparently, my thin skin scars easily.
A stray piece of grit creating not a pearl
but a red welt over my throat that
would need a scarf or necklace to head off nosy
'Have you had a tracheotomy?'
But over the last decade I have brazenly flaunted them,
with strappy tops and swimsuits.
Still catch nods and nudges
and the odd blatant enquiries, sniffing out scandal.
Know I should say 'mind your own business'
but no point trouncing rudeness with rudeness
so, Wikipedia response that leaves them none the wiser.
No time to fret anyway when so much life
to be had now. But catching myself in mirrors,
I notice they have, in fact, faded
with changing fortunes since you came along.

Best present ever

First year I am informed that
you 'Go to town at Christmas'
so, among the presents wrapped
with OCD perfection,
is the one you 'Paid over the odds for'
that whispers jeweller's presentation box,
and is opened with hot hands to reveal
the emerald and ruby of Turkish Delight.

Since then I have, like a firm guide dog, led you
towards suitable gifts, but this November
you trail 'I've cracked it this year.'
I keep the bar of my expectations low,
do raise an eyebrow at the sight of a
middle class man in our chav close,
ushered into the spare room,
who leaves baring a battered cardboard box.
slinging 'About two weeks' over his shoulder.

You inspect his work in silence,
come downstairs wreathed with a frown,
'Cost me a fortune and
He's botched part of the job.'
Apparently, 'the leather is tipsy.'

Sighs and headshakes as you cannot fully share
having sworn yourself to secrecy.
Nothing for it but to get your toolbox out.

Your swearing blasts like a flat sax,
as the thirsty wood drinks up the
glue with smacked lips,
leaving the leather insert flapping.
You emerge from an hour's soak in the bath
with a plan, decide to go all in with superglue,
that will require bomb disposal steady hands,
the jeopardy of one chance to get it right.
The house holds its breath until
your shrugged 'Well it's the best I can do.'

Touching enough that my wistful 'always wanted,'
when watching some antiques show, seeds in your mind.
But the labour of picking through websites,
the poker thrill of bidding online to win,
finding the furniture restorer who claims he can 'fix ,'
procuring the authentic desk leathering,
then the finishing flourish of sourcing squat ink wells,
makes this walnut writing slope,
daintily designed for the dimensions of a Victorian lady,
the belonging I would save if the house went up.

Mental Hack

I assumed my parent's legacy would be
death to feel my collar prematurely.
Inhabiting a body with a talent
for false alarms meant expecting the worst
became my best defence.
And middle age was an exotic destination
I never expected to visit.
But in my 50s you hand brake
turn my life and, giddy with fun,
I take my eye off the future, feast on the now,
dampened fears only occasional flaring,
you might be more trickster than saviour.

60th year all adventures are quarantined.
I kick around the days,
until pandemonium in my head.
Not the virus, but every twinge
whispering waking disease
that I am de-skilled at managing now.
To mark the day, pillion on your motorbike,
the scenery rushes by like life post 40.
Suddenly achieving sixty seems as
remarkable as all the other ways
I have outstripped my parents.
Then the gift of a mental hack,
'Everything now is extra.'

Trust

'You must trust him; he knows what he's doing.'
So, I wrench my eyes from on-coming cars,
avert my gaze as buses scrape past us,
look at the sky whilst you negotiate
doddery cycle riders,
allowing you to lead me in this riotous quick step.
Until, an argy bargy with white van on a roundabout,
I simply smile and shrug 'He'll sort it',
giggle as at traffic lights we weave past stationary
four-wheel drives as if waved through like VIPs.
'Follow his shoulder line on corners' and, at first,
I talk myself through each curve as if to a nervous child.
But over time offered the 'snaky or dual carriage way',
I choose the Herne Bay twists that, over the weeks,
we take lower and faster like our personal TT.
And sometimes we blast up the M2, doing a ton,
wind rattling my lid, battering my jacket,
In the wing mirrors, grinning at each other in cahoots.

Forgiveness

Telling that in childhood photos,
you look more like an evacuee billeted
on your family.

I see it was open season on you
after my dad's death, the brother-in-law
stitching you up proper.

Your face bringing all that trouble
tumbling down on you until you wished
you were plain.

Easy, I suppose, for the family to
cast you out then,
and brittle friendships break.

Fate certainly tied bad luck to your
tail, pitching you gutterwards,
your personality corkscrewing

as you saw the world
through a wine glass darkly,
your mothering becoming unmotherly.

But time for me to forgive,
because the fact is, even now,
I can't find the end to untangle -

Undertaking

(Previously published in The Cannon's Mouth Issue 86; December, 2022)

Ahead a dead 'Mr Badger'
dropped where struck on the road's crown.
Winced 'poor thing' imagining the suffering
which levels all animals.
Motorist's carefully skirt,
not wanting wheels to crush the creature
despite being beyond pain's catchment now.
I think of fetching a spade to stretcher
the body to the verge, for foxes
and buzzards to undertake the rest.

With humans, it's death's theft
of personality that's the difference,
what's left behind is a body
so uncannily empty,
we sigh with relief as the doors slam on
the private ambulance,
allowing the funeral director,
like a capable butler,
to smoothly usher
our squeamish thoughts away.
Happy enough later
to cast ashes upon the wind.

Closing the door
(Previously published in *Snakeskin*; September, 2022)

Now visits are more like incursions.
Her machine gun mouth rattling off a
magazine of family events, peppered with
rapid fire mockery of your accent and long hair.
After she leaves, I am scalded by the sight
of your eyes boiling with tears because I have
allowed us to become complicit in our own ridicule.

My instinct is to deface from memory this woman
who makes a lie of a childhood friendship.
But am persuaded that our 7-year-old selves
are strangers to us now, so leave intact the memory
of two kids whose imaginations collaborated
to create the fantastical worlds
we spent the summers lost in.
Until, at 14, she transformed from tomboy to vamp.
Siren sisters teaching her to play rough then,
first blood a spiteful prank played on a plainer teenager.

Later years a friendship with her mother.
Afternoons spent well, her dipping into a treasury
of anecdotes told with Joyce Grenfell verve.
Our laughter blown around the garden like bubbles.
And always space for me to speak of worries that rubbed,
her nurse's cumulated common sense
palliating what could not be cured.
In the wake of her funeral, I close the daughter's
front door firmly behind me.

Calling time
(Previously published in *Snakeskin*; September, 2022)

Our friendship cleaved for decades
over some nasty pranks now time eroded.
She suddenly barges back into my life,
model lean and with glamour that still gilds,
standing tall and straight as a sunflower,
a foot above me so I must look up to her.

Now used to chatter's gentle battledore
between friends made when more mature.
I find her words are one way traffic.
All her questions strictly rhetorical.
I wait for the window of an in breath
to insert a thumbnail of my own life,
manage to squeeze in some opinions
which she shreds and barnstorms on.

As kids we sped out her back door straight
into wonderland, told not to come back until late.
Then we lived for Planet of the Apes.
Now she assumes we share the same tastes,
but where she adores Hemmingway,
my preference is for 'The Great Gatsby'.
And when I tell her that I hate Elvis
she reacts as if I have punched her in the face.

In turn, I wince as she dismisses benefits as a free pass
for single mums with litters of kids to get a house,
shake my head when she damns social homes as weeds
sprouting up amongst crops of local new builds.
Until finally she reflects in undertone
'We have nothing now in common.'
And as if in mutual agreement our meetings
dwindle to chance chats in the street.

Happy go lucky
(Previously published in *The High Window;* May, 2023)

The gamble began in February when,
hands in pockets, signature whistle,
he would walk the orchards,
evaluating the blossoms' promise.
In March, the plain adolescent fruit
gave no hint of its eventual glamour,
but he could still estimate each cluster's count.

Always played his cards close to his chest
at the fruit auction, in the rear of the George pub.
Answered mates' 'What do you reckon Reg?'
with a knowing touch to the nose.
Staked all his savings on the fruit yield
with a wink. Afterwards, in the bar,
would raise a glass to kind weather.

In Spring, showers and sun collaborated
to plump and paint the fruit.
But in a wet summer's relentless rain
the cherries would fatten with water,
split their skins, rendering them unsaleable.

These years my grandfather would sit
on an empty box in a makeshift shelter,
shot gun primed at his feet,

not for suicide but thieving starlings,
who took the piss. Roll up in mouth
he would shake his head and grin at the cherries,
whose gashed flesh grinned back at him.
Canny enough to have laid off the bet though
with the hard fruit harvest,
Coxs and Conferences,
whose skins were tough as his hands.

And, seeing him through the winter,
contract pruning the same fruit trees.
Saw boning dead limbs, then deft
as a surgeon snipping just above buds.
Building up his stake money for next season's crop.
Winter evenings, he studied the Vauxhall catalogue,
suggested a Bournemouth B & B to grandmother,
if the gamble paid off the following year.

Missing Person
(Previously published in *The Journal;* winter, 2022

When good and bad strikes with equal force
I naturally burst to tell you first.

Second instinct is to phone the other one,
but find I can't call to mind, so shake my head

as if to loosen the memory of this person, tally friends
like someone missed off a Christmas card list,

but still can't identify, this one who will daft dance
around the kitchen at my good fortune,

takes any slight against me personally, and
suffers aftershock at my black luck.

Not a family member since my kin are all
rubbed out by death, and I am sibling less,

nor those kith whose friendships rotted from
the core with envy or some innocent effrontery.

I wonder if the mind is a universe where such memories,
although light years away, still shine dead star bright.

Or is this some saudade state for all those whose paths
peeled off from mine, either by death or design.

If I were naïve, a palm crossed with my credit card might
have me believe this person is about to arrive.

And philosophy, is maths with words. Ergo beyond me.
So, I am left scanning empty space for this somebody.

Monsters
(Previously published in *The High Window;* May, 2023)

Medusa and her kind not monsters born,
but beauties once and amiable even.
Just not knowing how to manage their talent,
and a propensity for foolish conduct.
Consequently, got lost in a maze
of wrong moves, with no oracular advice
from family members or friends.
Inevitable entanglement with the deities,
agents of fate, who threw spite in their faces,
laying waste, the superficial grace,
penetrating deeper than skin to corrode
their natures until monsters made.

Sickened by their own reflections,
they sobbed for their spoiled looks.
Solitary confinement on some remote rock,
they lost sight of the girl with the coquettish giggle,
burned with the realisation, no miraculous reversal
of their monstrous misfortune. No prospect of a hero
detouring their odyssey to rescue,
so threw themselves into perversion,
embraced every obscene compulsion.
The public chorus, like some salacious tabloid,
edited out the backstory, swelled the myth of her
with lip smacking headlines 'Monstrous Maneater'.

More than one way

We are confident our EQ like our IQ is above average.
After all, we wince at boxing matches on the TV,
routinely rattle tins for the local cat sanctuary,
and positively haemorrhage poems for refugees.

Oh, we still feel the same incendiary emotions,
love, hate, jealousy, anger, but our weapons
are smarter. Praise for instance is primed,
'How powerful,' 'to the many' 'very nice' to you.

In company, we cleave in half your sentences,
thrusting in our own opinions until your words
float away like lost balloons. Then we will close
the circle of our conversation against you.

And should you with dry mouth venture to
challenge us, we will suggest, with smirking eyes,
'You are too sensitive dear', for misreading
what we assure you is 'really just a bit of banter'.

From our vocabulary's arsenal we often select
words with multiple meanings that lure you
into misinterpretation, inferring your ignorance
with 'Oh, that's not what I meant at all.'

Expert at ambivalence, we lay our terms
like tripwires, their true meaning opaque
as our language, dancing on the cusp of cruelty,
so we can never be called out on it.

Like savvy heavies, our going overs leave
no physical evidence. We too are aiming
at internal injuries, but our bruises,
abrasions, bleeds will all be in your mind.

Ending

August, the robin swaps its song
to this slow bluesy tune, signalling
summer is slipping through my hands.
Not that I have squandered each day's glut of light.
Doors and windows have been left open
until evening inks the sky.
We have scrambled the bike at a moment's notice,
blasting off down to the coast.
Plums and cherries have been gorged on before
their season's small window slams shut.
I have stuffed the garden with flirty 'Hot lips '
whose tiny red lipsticked flowers
part to French kiss bees.
Now the wintry mood that was stashed away
with woollies in May stirs. I have no love for Autumn,
regard it as an arsonist putting a torch to trees
that are burnt out by November.
And even less for Winter when we must adjust again
to a life squeezed into shrunken days.
You have already entered next year's holidays
and events in the diary with bold black print.
Whereas I have learned to only pencil in the future.

Time out

Hardly the best hotel view yet
even building sites offer colour here.
No safety helmets, but conical Berber hats,
woven from reed, at odds with knock off
Gucci tee shirts and Levi jeans.
Each 2 and 3 man crew knows their task,
is hard at it in a constant percussion
of sawing and hammering.
No second glance from co- workers
towards one man still as an Anthony Gormley figure,
a clue lying in the dusty rug unfurled at his feet.
Commences with a symbolic dry washing of the face,
then the body's elegant
swoop onto the knees and onwards
to bob his forehead in obeyance,
all the while incanting in undertone.
Carrying within the calm of the mosque,
his mind is sound proofed against
screeching motor bikes, locals with no volume control.
Time travels to a 10-minute preview
of the future he expects to receive.
I have no such ritual that will admit
my mind to a place of sanctuary, where cares
that pester like blow flies are silenced.
It's medication must seek to do that job.

Ambush

We stride up avenues that seem to unroll before us.
Looking at watches, plunge across free for all roads.
Finally flop on café chairs, order, and wait as night
cancels the day like a blind drawn down.

One Adhan triggers another until all four fling
voices to the sky, their vaulting vocals extraordinary
as tenors, temporarily cutting off the snake charmers,
grating clarinets and stall holders harsh cries.

Like opera the foreign tongue makes for pure sound.
And, akin to a tenor's top C, always ambushes me,
penetrates my secular worship of stuff to gift a moment
of sublime I answer with the sweet smart of tears.

Old School

We gather at the old school's wake,
before the bulldozers dispatch.
As teachers and ex-pupils pass in corridors
there are familiar traces in faces, but no names.
Their grown-up gaze is brazen, whilst our eyes
snatch away, embarrassed by time's edit.
In the hall, pupils rifle through year books.
Memory is a time machine, transporting
them back to teens, defaulting to nick names,
guffawing at mug shots. Old friendship groups reform
as they invade form rooms, their own kids trailing
behind as parents temporarily become strangers.

Strapping Jack the lads seek out teachers,
not to settle old scores, but extend hands:
'Just wanted to say thank you, Sir.'
Other pupils reminisce until memory runs dry,
Tactful 'Well lovely to see you again '
cues not to overstay the moment.
Mostly students have made a go of life,

premium cars attesting to their success.
But as for the teachers - a maths master
gamely copes as dementia steals his wife.
Two suicides; one who touched forbidden fruit,
the other, mourning the career she gave 40 years to.

My first and best post, fond memory
has distorted the school's dimensions,
now the hall appears abbreviated,
the cafeteria has gobbled itself up,
and the sixth form common room's teenage squalor
has been routed by board room order.
But the boys' humour, the girls' sass has not been
augmented by nostalgia. Nor the staff room of characters
who would find no place in the new school,
with its curriculum Hard Times dry, delivered by
sharp suited staff bearing corporate smiles.
A pound buys our names etched on a window,
memorialising past teachers who once
had a passion to pass on their passion.

Circus

Months sequestered like light house keepers,
we now have box set, books, and baking fatigue.
A jaunty flyer trumpets the promise of 'Santus Circus'.
Both of us crave entertainment with a pulse.
Queuing up, we find courtesy is back in fashion,
with smiles and *sorry* and leaving spaces.

Childless, our first visit since childhood,
we find clowns are suave now in waistcoat and jeans,
raffish face paint unlikely to engender night terrors,
throwing only buckets of charm at the audience.
And the girls, no simpering in sequins and feathers,
but thrilling on the trapeze, strutting on the high wire.

Parents have brought stir crazed kids,
who look up open mouthed at acrobats performing
superhuman stunts created not by CGI
but hours of pain and practice.
Of course, they will desert when the multiplexes,
with plush seats and popcorn, reopen.

Increasingly, in the housing gold rush,
new builds lay claim to fallow fields,
circuses struggle for sites, find themselves
marginalised, prevented from flaunting
their footloose life in our 9 to 5 faces,
tempting kids to escape exams rut and run away to join.

Strange, circuses never adopted by the retro crowd,
perhaps regarded as a little too groundling.
Inevitably these contortionists are fated to work
call centres, jugglers flip burgers and jaunty big tops
become permanently tethered in vintage photos,
served up as nostalgia on bijou coffee shop walls.

Toy Run
(Previously published in *Grey Sparrow Press* issue 43; July, 2023)

The youngster in lime leathers
on champing Kawasaki
boasts immortality as bike and
biker become a roadblock, holding back
two snarling lanes of traffic.
So we, on this motorcycle run for charity,
may pass like a fast-flowing river.
First time perhaps as an out-rider,
he busily buzzes by the main procession
of some 300 experienced bikers.
Gets a thumbs up from me in
tribute to his fearlessness.
I know at 69 you ache to slew
our big old tourer across a double lane,
in a 'You shall not pass' attitude,
wearing an expression grim as death.
But my clenched muscles scream
don't you dare as, at 62,
I feel the hot breath of mortality
on the back of my neck.

'White Christmas'

When the Christmas Eve snow silenced the traffic
that screamed through our village,
mother and I, stolen chocolate and
frowning school report forgotten,
trespassed with present opening thrill
into the middle of the highway
and, thumbing our noses at the muzzled motors,
danced with Isodora Duncan abandon,
accompanied by the wild flurry
of an agitated snow globe.
Then, organic as a musical,
I suddenly began to trill
'I am the lord of the dance'.
the gold of mother's 'How clever you are',
as if I'd spontaneously composed
the drilled piece from my school's repertoire.
Catching the song, she and I sang and danced
in the harmony of our own 'White Christmas'.

Last Rites

I went to Boots from habit, selecting Rimmel
because neither of us ever used the brand.

The undertaker led me into the grisly Santa's Grotto,
then stood sentinel to reassure.

At first sight shock, mother appeared to have
been snatched by grave robbers.

Would never have chosen to be seen dead in the white gown
that suggested she was marrying death itself.

A daughter's final duty now to protect her from
prying eyes that might pay a peep show visit.

Striking up a one-sided conversation, like a
hairdresser with a darkly quiet client,

I forced fingers to dab make up on the stiffened flesh,
clammy to the touch, tolerating for ten minutes.

But now the cosmetic alchemy failed to conjure
up her face, casting instead the indelible image

That my mother had sunk into a profound sulk.

Fear of letter boxes

I listen all morning for the letter boxes'
snapped warning, my pen skids across a page.
Careering downstairs I scan the door mat,
gingerly poke a pile of junk mail where buff
envelopes often lurk like adders under compost.
If found I open as if defusing a bomb.
Seeing a drift of white letters,
I down grade my fear to code orange,
knowing even these are not always as
innocent as they appear.
Sometimes, the friendly face of familiar handwriting,
or an invitation, surprising as a modest lottery win.
Still no 'all clear' by 12 o'clock,
I peep from curtains,
catching the post man passing my gate,
exhale as if missed out of a
house to house search.
Sundays, strikes and snow,
I am a school kid whose bully
has been excluded for a few days.

Midwinter Monday

A heron grey sky all day,
when nature seems agnostic
about Spring's resurrection.
Each pub we find is mothballed
during the week. We persevere down
B roads that are narrow as minds,
waltzing the car around pits and pocks
that would take out a tyre.
Easier to contact the dead
than get a signal on your phone,
we pray no oncoming traffic,
as pull- ins are sticky with mud.

Each strike at conversation fails
like damp matches, until silence
creeps into our mouths.
20 years friendship banked,
we have no need to fake fun.
Eventually settle at Faversham,
a tumble weed town on Mondays.
In a café, door open to welcome
the chill, we are the sole customers.

Sandwiches and coffee manage
to fuel low burner chat.
We slag off the government and Putin.
But our usual gallows humour
is slack as an empty jib.
We have had such misfire days before,
like that time at Brighton races,
when the rain pissed on us all afternoon.
And as a pair of melancholics, we rather
relish this day's pathetic fallacy.

Letter

The letter was perched upon the end of year flotsam,
washed up on my desk. Formally attired in an envelope,
'Miss Sinclair' addressed in neat script.

Inside, two brimming pages of A4,
unblemished by scratching out so must have been
rehearsed before this fair copy.

Its author, one of those year 11,
life and soul of the classroom lads,
who always knuckled down when told.

Turns out for the two years where most kids
view GCSE literature as a means to an end,
he had learned to read humanity between its lines.

Particularly, my banging the feminist drum loud enough
to drown out the snickering of schoolboys, who believed
Eva Smith 'Enjoyed going on the game'.

Thanks, given for straightening out a skewed view
of women, inherited from male family members.
Closet Feminist now, he knew to treat women right.

As to my personal qualities, his tone was courtly,
his sentiments chaste as the white paper he wrote upon.
But it was, I realised, a love letter of sorts.

Couple of years on, I spotted him strutting the concourse
of a shopping mall with his mates, loud with life.
A second's recognition, then his attention flicked

back to pals. I took the cue, feigned interest in a shop
window; understanding the jeopardy of greeting an old
English tutor amongst chums for whom teachers

were either the enemy or irrelevant. Perhaps, too, he had
written in the amnesty of the last days at school, when
scores good and bad can be settled without come-back.

Why I don't write about refugees
(Previously published in *The Shot Glass Journal*; May, 2022)

No doubt it's well meant, but their Dachau dark stories
are beyond even our fecund imagination
so attempts at writing them are mere ventriloquism.
As exploitative, perhaps, as the traffickers
who sell promises at premium rates.
Our duty is to bear the rub of our own impotence,
watching from sofas the squalor of camps where inmates
with empty faces live in the awful limbo of now.
And as the TV news dishes up with dinner the shocking
scramble for boats designed for pleasure, not plight,
it should be too much for our conscience to swallow.
Better to wait for their voices to be restored
and memories recovered so they can tell their own tales,
albeit in a borrowed tongue.

Aging

Since my parents left no blueprint,
old age is inventing me as we go along.
Making up in the mirror, mind elsewhere,
I overlook time's subtle siphoning of my youth.
Except some days, notice a sad clown
sagging of the mouth as I apply lipstick.
But sometimes, in the passenger seat,
full sunlight offers no soft focus, as wicked
wing mirrors find my face's worst angles,
and I avert my eyes from age spots as I
once swerved my gaze from acne.

An impulse to self-efface from photos
where all sides are bad now,
or hand shield 'No photos' like a diva.
But it's not as if I am a great beauty,
whose assets are being stripped with time.
And when half my life is already unrecorded,
neither sepia baby snaps,
nor teenage shots in booths,
each photo is a flag planted in borrowed time,
after all no knowing how far
I will be allowed to tip-toe into old age.

46

Manly Hugs

Lunchtime, builders swarm
the supermarket snack counter,
loud and brash as starlings,
their livery high vis jackets, dusty overalls,
grimy fingers grasping pies and energy drinks,
ambidextrously handing over cash
whilst chatting up the cashier.
One is snagged by a civilian chum,
needy for blokey catch up. Separating,
they hug 'Nice to see you mate'.
I think of my dad, working on the farm,
habitually shod in wellies, jumpers like gouda cheese,
whose pals from school, cricket, farming,
packed the pews at his memorial.
Men ranked above mum and me,
rarely treated to a peck or pat.
Friends who would have dodged a manly
hug like a punch, preferring the comfortable
distance of a handshake's space.

Pillion

The bike roars off with rock and roll riff.
Troubles are stuffed in my jacket pockets as I scan
for traffic lights, junctions, anti-bikers,
brace on foot pegs and sissy bar for the shunt.
Some malicious roads hide ruts in shadows,
whip out last minute to wind me, I adjust with a wriggle.
Others flaunt their pocked surfaces that you
skirt the bike around, my hips responding in
Samba figure of eight. And bends we embrace like fate.
But on trustworthy roads, I am free to watch the
zoetrope landscape; a brooding donkey in a field,
spooked sheep scattering at the bike's snarl,
and once a flight of finches flying alongside for fun.
The two-hour trip seems brief as a fair ground ride.
Nevertheless, we return giddy with wellbeing,
my pockets picked by the wind.

The decorators have left for good

The packet withers in the bathroom cabinet.
I know that most women, after decades
of hieroglyphics on the calendar and condom diplomacy,
gather pills, caps, towels,
and fling them in the dustbin.
'Good riddance'.

But I miss the womb's monthly husbandry,
an excuse for pit bull rage at shop girls
shoddy service, gorging on snickers and crisps,
even the niggle of mosquito cramps,
until the first flow has the body sighing
with relief.

My twenties forfeited,
I scurried through education and career,
expecting to win a husband like a prize
in a competition I hadn't entered
until, at 50, I find my body
has deducted every month
from the allocation of fecundity
I thought infinite,
so, Roberta and Oliver will remain fiction.

Words fail

Sometimes our language is tongue tied.
Dictionaries are at a loss to give a definition.
Our analogies fail to find a comparison.
Even the best words are a monkey's chatter.

Aboriginal words must give relief,
unalloyed with casual use by lazy tongues,
their violent utterance ripped from throats,
like screams to arouse a primitive understanding.

We need a new language, held in reserve,
loaned to us only when events slip the
leash of ordinary words and bolt beyond
the reach of common understanding.

Pristine words, with distilled meaning,
engendering a supernatural communication
which we must use responsibly.
Until then, there is the anti-language, silence.

Clock

Thirty silent clocks:
estate of an elderly man
who hoarded time in his bungalow
until each piece was spent
and he became time bankrupt.
I choose one for its looks,
wind it up like an old-fashioned toy,
smile at its resuscitated 'tick-tock'.
But, on my mantlepiece,
it clamours above TV and chat,
raising its voice when I leave the room,
forcing me to heed each second's death.
Then every five hours, stops.

Still Human

Each week dull Tesco trips brightened
by a fresh motor on the cusp of their land.
Hipster catnip of camper or convertible,
competitively priced, 'Engine extra' we would chuckle.

That Tuesday, pulsing police lights
smack of a raid on the encampment.
Even a squad car sentinel on the central verge.
Whatever the story, we root for the travellers.

Evening news tells a grizzly tale. How, in the early hours
mother and sister, bearing balloons and birthday banners,
entered brother's burger van to deck, lit the generator,
carbon monoxide making the space a gas chamber.

Middle class chums are niggardly with their condolence,
yet ready enough to spend sympathy on migrants,
as if people who park their lives on the margins
do not share their complete colour chart of emotions.

Next week, desolation hangs over the site like low cloud.
Caravans crowd the entrance, ponies have vanished.
Developers previously seen off now rub their hands
at the prospect of this piece of prime land.

But some months later, a dumper truck is up for sale,
OVNO, suggesting might take a bullseye off for cash.
And the site, caravans and their animal retinue are back,
as the travellers flourish one finger up to luck.

Table

It's the parlour table I keep returning to,
assuming they would work in solitude,
a bedroom, attic, sitting room.
But it was here they put down needles to pick up pens,
sometimes pacing around it to stretch minds and legs,
reading out next instalments for sisterly frankness,
faith in each other's judgement like a trust fall.
I shake my head at the image of the novels
written a table width away from each other,
making them the best writing group ever.
It's the extraordinary odds too,
of not one genius sibling but three.
A darker inheritance also,
as their brilliant minds seemed
to mortgage their bodies' strength.

My father was

A man's man who, finding himself saddled
with a wife and daughter, routinely chose
cricket, football, strip joints over us.

Work days unreachable on the farm,
like a spy in the field, employers were in cahoots,
putting off the scent.

His crepuscular return greeted by our dog
waiting at the gate, whose ecstasy of capering
father skirted without acknowledgment .

At 40, he held onto life as if waiting
for an eleventh-hour reprieve from
a cancer death sentence that never came.

Afterwards, my mother's wide eyed
widow's progress that descended
into an Hogarthian end.

Years of her assassinating his character
means I have torn up, like old photographs,
most memories of my father.

Dining amongst the dead

As the trickle of worshipers dried,
the chapel was sold off to developers
who converted sympathetically.
However, no garden, since old bones
cannot be evicted like squatters.
Family plots bare old village names,
still extant amid the influx of newcomers.
Graves maintaining social segregation,
landowners with handsome memorials
in prime positions, whilst labourers consigned
to dark corners. Separation, too, between
certain families who bear a feud into the afterlife.
The old car park becomes a makeshift patio,
tables and chairs suggesting al fresco dining,
beside the remains of death's great feasting.
Graveyard grass is kept under, but ecumenical law
also precludes removing moss clad tombstones,
so stacked against walls like a grim garden feature.
Baronet peers over baker, Hogben elbows Wanstall,
an eternity now to settle their differences.

Bowing

Five years since its clearance,
the garden remains disputed land.
Nature's guerrilla struggles to rewild,
my striving to fashion a cottage garden.

Spring incursions, nagging common sense,
'Bend from the knees' 'Use a kneeler', is
ignored as prolonging chores. So, doubling over,
I plunge my grumbling body into undergrowth.

The small of my back screams as I straighten
up to inspect handiwork. Decide to stay stooped,
tackle the pain later, in one hit. Thereafter move
around the garden like a lower case 'r'.

Hour and half later, I ease up with caution.
Kneading my back, see beyond ancient roses
to my late grandmother, whose own crooked stance
I once smiled at, but have inherited with this garden.

Her peasant wisdom, learned the hard way,
picking up potatoes all day. Minimising the wear
and tear on a body that must last her 80 years.
Now, across time, we bow to each other.

Reflex

Even now, when routinely passing,
my gaze is still caught by the lane
where rhododendrons once teased
with glimpses of the reclusive cottage.

Despite seeing with my own eyes its fate.
How the builder's hands, tied by grade 11 listing,
pulled down what was too far gone and, as if in peak,
bolted on a brutalist extension.

But in memory I can still walk the house,
where light peered through lead paned windows,
to be mitigated by the family's gilded glamour.
Stroke dust from a statue with a story,

scan Hemmingway's that signalled 'intellect'.
The dazzle of it all, casting into shadows
memories of my own childhood home
where, in comparison, life always seemed a little less.

New

Initially we watched telly on one sofa .
Held hands like teenagers until
sundered by your back pain.
Now we are adrift on separate settees,
a 4 ft straight of carpet between us.
Despite your body healing,
an unspoken understanding
that the comfort of lounging full length
on couches has become habit now.

But on the motor bike,
when railway crossings halt our journey,
you cut the engine,
settle back against me,
in a different kind of coupling
which, despite dense leathers,
is close as skin on skin.
I prop my chin on your shoulder
as we chat in this new intimacy.

Sheffield Steel

Even in the 70s Sheffield's steel crucible
forged only macho men.
So you witness protected your identity
behind long strides in black Doc Martens,
wiping dirty hands-on brown overalls,
hunching over roll ups in navy donkey jacket.
But weekends deployed gay spy-craft:
whispered Polari,
keys coyly slung from belt loops,
gold neck-chain's glint,
leading to stomach churning cottaging in gents,
palm prickling pick- ups in blind eye pubs,
heart racing rendezvous in suburban bedsits.
Hastily pulling back on your butchness
for the late bus home,
drunken lads still saw beneath
to the pansy, queer, fairy
crouching inside and dealt with you.

Then the flit to London, in Soho's sanctuary,
released inner camp gene genie,
with nature kohled eyes, mocha skin, lean body,
you swanked in tight white tops and tight white jeans,
watering mouths following your Marilyn wiggle
down Old Compton Street.
And shaking your booty in 'Bang'
added rock star notches to your bed post.
Kept your tongue Sheffield steel sharpened
as you deposed killer Queens.
Outside the Soho ghetto still set upon on underground,
but took your beating with 'Whatever' bravado.

And weekends, in 6-inch pink diamante stilettos,
scarlet mini dress, Blondie wig,
you waved your purple feather Boa in society's face,
sprinting across the concourse of Victoria Station
en route to find heaven in 'Heaven'.

Banning Barbie

My mother banned pneumatic Barbie.
Despite topping my every gift list,
closest I got was the toyshop shelves,
the dolls lined up like a beauty pageant.
And that, for her, was the issue.

Amongst the midden of my father's
mini pick up, page 3 girls with similar assets.
Mother was skinny, legacy of a wartime childhood,
who despite a dark, fierce beauty,
found gentlemen still preferred buxom blondes.

But I see Barbie as a last-ditch effort
to teach little girls to be biddable
and vacant as Stepford wives,
whilst women's liberation hacked through
the chains of the kitchen sink.

Today, we are told, her wardrobe
encourages bolder aspirations.
But still no disguising those bold breasts
beneath an astronaut suit, and a barrister's wig
cannot contain that billowing blonde hair.

Now a feature film persuades pink clad audiences,
brandishing matching manikins,
that their girl has turned feminist now.
So sisters' see as empowerment the self-editing
that recreates them in Barbie's image.

Maxwell's silver hammer

Solo ride out and a white van
sees you as sport, buzzes from behind,
overtakes then sharply cuts you up,
only experience keeps the bike from
slewing across the road.

Eyes stoked with mischief
you confess, always ride 'tooled up',
the slim but sturdy hammer tucked
inside a quick draw pocket.
Throwback to the bad land 70s.

You give chase until, riding adjacent,
one hand on the accelerator,
the other draws the hammer, smashes
the van's side window like peanut brittle,
brakes scream; you are a speck on the horizon.

Your revelation briefly shakes
like the boom of distant ordnance.
But I choose to marvel at your stunt rider skill,
train my anger on the van driver
who casually conspired to make me a widow.

Yet this exploit reminds that getting to
the bottom of anyone is like
fathoming the universe with the naked eye.
And I admit there are even times when
I become a stranger to myself.

Oakworth Station

The train's arrival is the clapperboard cue
for another middle-aged woman
to recreate the film's scene.
Not the giddy romance of Brief Encounter,
but that fierce first love for a father.
The happy accident of the actress's words
reverberates in endless echo down the generations,
the frequency touching every girl who watches,
so that tears spring to the surface.
The simple phrase 'my daddy'
perhaps recalling first words.
The scene cuts all daughters keenly,
many mourn dads who fell for them at first sight,
others yearn for the fathers that might have been.

Wonderland

Illuminated photographs of lilies
invite us to drown our sorrows.
Economy of space means comfy seats
are placed uncomfortably close.
Beside me is a woman whose bulk
is not loss of control but a massing of strength.
She is painted in colours that nature
warns are dangerous;
aggravated by a comedy hat.
In her urgency to organise
her weekly medication,
she overwhelms a small table,
loudly tabulating her days.
On my right is a man dressed
elegantly to disguise his status,
who betrays himself with a
monologue into a mobile.
Suddenly, he demands more than
silent agreement from his listener.
Instinctively half turning his body
in a cue for privacy, he extorts loyalty
with the clichéd line 'I can't do this on my own',
that seems inadequate to his demand,
but he charges it with a tone of ferocious despair
that carries a threat to them both.
This is a waiting room for patients whose
afflictions have turned them inside out.
Despite the walls attempts at tranquillity
our symptoms, like unruly pets,
will not be house trained.

Internet dating

At first my 'best side' photo is mobbed by men
so feel like Scarlett O'Hara at a ball, until I discover lads
seeking carefree cougar sex
or a meal ticket,
and from my own demographic;
inquiries after my hosiery,
and panting mobile numbers.

I search through my matches past Kray twin lookalikes,
married men wearing tell-tale dark glasses,
sad self-portraits with bed sit back grounds,
for the handful of guys I might accept a drink from.

Beginning to e-flirt with grin and wink emoticons,
over the week I virtual two time
men from Rochester and Deal,
who bus stop chat about work and their tea,
neither making the gear change up to seduction.

Difficult, I suppose, for most blokes
who barely scrawl a birthday card for mum
to strike a balance between
'Hello Sexy' or 'It's raining here',
and write me into bed with Casanova craft.

Terms of endearment

At first, I bask in his 'darling' and 'sweetheart',
believing them monogamous.
Then deflate with disappointment
at his promiscuous 'thank you sweetheart'
to some shop assistant.
But, in time, I learn that 'dearest'
in his daily text is sent with dictionary worth.

Whereas, in return, I cough up a 'love',
slur over a 'honey',
mumble a 'dear',
words alien to me
as 'fuck' and 'bollocks' are to others.

And in response to his 'I love you',
uttered with a child's spontaneity,
I find the words have rusted in my mouth.

Lucky Streak

You divine the fortunes of each horse
like a sorcerer and his almanac,
whilst I play hand bag top trumps
with passing women.
At the bookies' window I avert my eyes
from your stake in pin number etiquette,
place a pound each way on a
name that takes my fancy.
The winnings rain coins like a slot machine payout.
By the third race you regard me as if
Satan is my tipster. 'Pick another',
I close my eyes and jab at the heraldry
of jockeys' silks.
While men in bespoke suits and women
in Chanel bray, we watch with sniper coolness
as my horse glides to victory.
You urge me to ride my luck
but I am still expecting it to run dry.
Nevertheless, leave carrying a bag ripe with cash.
Silence on the drive home as you calculate
the odds that, fantastic as light years,
I have defied this afternoon.
I ignore your parting plea to
'play the lottery this once'.
Now a suspicion that my life's allocation
of good fortune paid out in a single dividend that day.

Satan spends Sunday at a boot sale

His devil's face is like a prank played
with indelible ink by mates as he dozed,
but hair trained into two budding horns,
whole body pigmented toadstool red,
suggests he savours with theatrical relish
the shudders, shaken heads, stares that follow
his Sunday stroll with wife and grandkids,
and an inward 'Ha! Ha! Ha!'
as stall holders pray, he won't pause
to browse for tools, electrical goods, souls.

Of course, the real Satan would disguise himself
as the grey-haired gent in beige fleece, brown cords,
twinkling as his table is mobbed by women
eager for his home-grown organic apples.

The Quiet Room

We wince under the waits added load.
Squashed seating arrangements anticipate
breasts squeezed into scanners.
We are blind to fresh flowers, pastel walls.
Receptionists and nurses maintain cheeriness
of shopping channel presenters but
fear runs amok amongst us,
strangling our instinct to chat.
The pages of 'Hello' are turned with shaking hands,
eyes skim bikini clad celebs,
whilst we strain for a bustling nurse to pop her head
around the door and sing our name.
A girl in Sainsbury's uniform nuzzles
her boyfriend's shoulder.
It must be confusing for men,
this switch from 'Carry On' fondling to
reluctantly tracing a lump insidious as an IED.
We watch other women liberated by
'Every thing's fine you can go'.
But for one woman, the nurse in sotto voce voice,
'Would you come through to the quiet room?'
We imagine boxes of tissues and the private exit.
15 minutes trudge by. 'For God's sake'
I re-cross legs, switching my coat about me.
Finally discharged, I scurry from the building,
high on relief. Slam the car door this time on the nurse
with the Valium voice and her open invitation
for me to join her in 'that room'.

Second Wind

Retiring at 65, you get a second wind.
Your mornings are tinkering.
Your afternoons are feet up watching classic 90s TV.
At Aintree, your black Crombie
with a flash of red shirt draws
'You look cool man' tributes
from booted and suited lads;
and your trade mark hair, splendid as a crest,
has older men smoothing bald-pates
and sighing 'Nice cut mate.'

At 59, I am winded by five months
repeating revision litany to private pupils
at vespers hour; bingeing in the car on Snickers
for sugar spike to keep my eyes open;
carrying my weight gain with the shame
of a 1950s unmarried mother.
At the Grand National, all I can throw together
is beige shift dress, dun coat, grey hat,
a pheasant hen's dowdy plumage.

Whilst you glide on the current
of such compliments,
I flap behind,
trying with wing-clipped confidence
to keep up with you.

Day Tripper

At first a horror film thrill at the razor wire
garlanding the hospital.
Sat in the waiting room holding my breath
beside the other out patients,
who were unexploded bombs liable to go off 'BANG'.
Scrabbled in my bag for a book as defence
against the man in rumpled clothes
who tossed random phrases at me like a lonely kid
trying to entice someone to play ball with him.
Looked up eagerly each time a consultant
greeted their client with the impeccable manners
of a maître d' overlooking the foibles
of the very wealthy.
But after several appointments,
my therapist and I would remark upon the weather
whilst navigating the hospital's computer game
of locked doors and forbidden levels.
In the coffee bar watched with animal indifference
as the in-patient assistant slowly calculated
her change as if it was foreign currency.
Ate sandwiches in the grounds, watching squirrels caper,
occasional screams issuing from acute wards
indigenous as the cry of sea gulls by the coast.

Family Portrait

This old carrier contains the remains
of a jumbled family jigsaw, whose puzzle
lies in the telltale outline of vanished lives.

A few of you went underground, lay in wait,
until distracted hands, digging in drawers,
disinterred eyes that still could not be met.

Time travelling back through tiny windows
of history, even faces estranged by youth
remain as potent as their owner's presence.

Strange suddenly to find this platonic version of you
surviving on untarnished in the memory of your friend.
Here, you are innocent of the people you became.

Slower than growth, some of you are allowed to
creep back, given temporary lodgings in shadows,
house ghosts whom we must learn to live with.

When a sex symbol takes to sensible shoes

Suddenly, across the store, through a middle aged
bottle glass blur, I spot blonde hair familiar as a logo,
but hesitate, unable to make out that fantasy body
drawn by an adolescent boy on his exercise book.
Close up, these photographs from the 'Misfits' are like
meeting an old friend after a debilitating illness.
Trademark eyeliner has become heavy shutters closing
on empty windows of a house whose occupant has left.
Her body still forms a perfect 8 but is not gift wrapped in
gold lamé, instead she is a hillbilly's wife in white cotton
Sunday dress, posing in a Steinbeck farm yard.
Looking down the barrel of the camera, lips no longer
part in the throes of an orgasmic O,
but are forced into a localised smile.
The confection of a single 1950s picture draws my eyes
like wasps to a baker's window, leaving me craving
other heyday poses, addictive as sugar.
Paying my last respects to the stills from her final film
I notice, more shocking than being shared around like a
joint by the Kennedy boys' club, her comfortable shoes.

Synchronised Swimming
(Previously published in *Snakeskin* 295; February,2022)

Launching into the sea, you flip on
your back and float like flotsam.
Behind I wade waist high, bracing against
waves that buffet and barge me.
Positioning yourself to blunt
the worst of the waves,
you coax me like a toddler.
Breathless false starts – gasping half strokes,
my legs never fully committing.
After each failure, I chide
'if you can get on the back of a motor bike-'
Success is a few rushed strokes,
until I run out of bottle and breathe,
my feet groping for the seabed again.

Leaving me in baby-pool shallows;
on a sunbed your concentration
is cleaved between a Rebus thriller and my antics
as I practice thrashed sequences of strokes
that you reward with the odd thumbs up.
Late afternoon the sea naps;
I find its tranquillity infectious,
we swim abreast in grown up depths,
me every now and then dropping my toe
like a tiny anchor to skim the sea floor.

And there is something elemental
in this synchronised experience
that is novel to me, but you take for granted.
Wading shoreward,
I laugh and gasp superlatives,
perhaps because I no longer fear
that you will swim away from me.

A game of hide and seek

My last chip, this London hospital,
clinical records given the slip somewhere in Kent.
A scribbled note from my GP,
I sat before this consultant
with a newborn's medical history.
Lottery numbers excitement as he nodded
at my narrative, flourish of his fountain pen
and I was entombed in an MRI machine.
When my tight-lipped body
foiled his lines of enquiry,
'I think we'll keep an eye on you'.
Knowing some disorders play
a game of hide and seek.
Writing degree essays in the waiting room
gave way to marking kids' homework.
As check-ups routinely reassured me,
'I don't think there's anything to worry about'
So, for years I didn't.

Future conditional
(Previously published in *Obsessed with Pipework* 97; February 2022)

Newscasts start it with what seem at first
Sci-fi years, 2035, 2040, 2050 but, on reckoning,
I find they are like deadlines, closer than I think,
and totalling them to my current age,
these dates would find me at 80,90, nothing.
I redo the maths, but the figures are adamant,
making my future like a dwindling fortune.
If lucky I have about 20 years' worth left,
and at 60 I know decades gather momentum now.
No fear of death as such since we have had an
on off relationship since childhood.
But like the metamorphosis from
acne afflicted adolescent to a passable
young woman with a knack for make-up,
now in the near distance the final transmutation
from well preserved middle age to undeniable old lady.
Sometimes, my mirror previews with downturned
Emoji mouth and bags under the eyes, not designer,
that can no longer be dismissed as tiredness.
In my twenties, the prospect of 40 made me wince,
much like 80 does today. The difference then was coming
into a trust fund of time, I could afford to blow.
Now I cannot squander years, as life has me on notice.

Mr. Turner's dimmer switch

Some pictures we peer into paint affray,
as if trying to make sense of catastrophe.
Must take his titular word about
figures, objects, landscapes.
But we do not give up with shake of head,
or dismiss with shrug and walk on.
Instead, calmly face the storm's black heart
until, stealthily, our patience begins to pay out
as yellow and white low lights
begin to illuminate the gloom,
revealing the truth of flailing boats, struggling figures.
Whispered 'Do you see?' You corroborate
in a tone usually reserved for virtuoso engineering.
'It's like a dimmer switch being turned on.'
'How does he do it?' We recall the cabinets,
displaying annotated text books on colour-optics.
Knowledge that biology is working
behind the scene here does not diminish in our opinion.
Rather, as we struggle to grasp oil slippery concepts
that slide through our comprehension,
we remain awe struck by this art-science alchemy.

Ephemeral

Occasionally, life throws me a double six day:
a birthday perhaps, that I Eeyore predicted
would be bottom of the pile in everyone's busy lives.
Then champagne giddy at the carefully chosen words
of husband's card that Cyrano speak for him.
Giggle as one chum sings 'Happy Birthday' down the
phone, despite both being in our 50s.
Beam at the friend on my front door step who bears
purple orchids like a giant corsage.
And I continue to unwrap this day
like a lingering game of pass the parcel,
where the music stops at me every time.
And on this day, I do not fire off one finger to the driver
who cuts me up, instead a 'Whatever' shrug.
No 'Fuck You' is detonated by the shop assistant who
holds my purchase hostage until ID is shown,
instead. a beatific smile.
Such days, however always lapse at midnight.
The following morning, a reckoning,
as I ache with anti-climax,
my mood slumping as if for a little death.

Tattoo Tabular Rasa

Modest tattoos are mainstream
as make up now.
Rose bud peeping from sleeve,
flash of heart on midriff,
snake sunbathing on bikini shoulders
all elicit squeals from teenage girls,
desperate to be 18.
No longer the brand of a tart
But, like saucy underwear,
an acceptable tramp stamp hint
hidden in saucy parts of
MPs, DRs, lawyers.
And for midlife baby boomers,
crisis equivalent to husband's Harley.
Some tattoos have deeper
than skin significance though.
C section gash, cellulite, stretchmarks
are tattoo trounced by
children's names, butterflies, curlicues.
Others use cancer remission 'carpe diem',
post-divorce phoenix, to write their future
on skin like a refreshed tabula rasa.

Side Effects

The meds not only supress orgasm,
but that other head-thrown-back,
body-heaving pleasure, laughter.
Anxious your joke does not tumbleweed
across the table, I stretch my lips
into smiled 'That's a good one',
or in raucous company, where banter battle cocks
force laughter painful as pneumonia's breath.
Sometimes the real thing will suddenly gift;
bent double at false moustaches in pound shop,
binge giggle at Eddie Izzard gig.
A yearning though for a daily dose
of spontaneous giggles, belly laughs, guffaws,
whose side effects switch off pain
more efficiently than Co-codamol,
lifts depression higher than Prozac.

Grief

After the hearse glissades up to the entrance
a hiatus, as immediate family members mill.
The rest of us have congregated
at an un-obtrusive distance,
like extras waiting for our cue.
Spotting the collage of our familiar faces
she abandons funeral protocol,
and leaving the undertakers discretely
checking their watches,
begins to greet us individually.
I turn my head as her tears haemorrhage,
un-staunched by tissues,
because I can never remember
seeing her cry, even as a kid.

Reaching his prognosis' end game,
his death still felled her like a stroke.
No personal call this time, as when her father,
the first love of her life, died.
No 'Buck up' pep-talk to herself,
in this family who pride themselves
on never being 'mimsy'.

Instead, her sisters made arrangements.
And my communication with her
over the previous few weeks ,
a few eggshell texts,
a row of kisses.

But now I see that she grieves
as passionately as she loves,
lost for the words that usually come
like eager dogs at her bidding,
her gratitude for our attendance
is conveyed in ardent hugs.
Finding myself ambushed by this break
from funeral etiquette,
I return the pressure of her embrace,
like for like, croak a few words,
as if attempting a foreign language.
When she moves on, my anxiety stands down,
and I can look at her now.
Strange in black, since she always prefers 'brights'
to match her primary-colour personality.
Yet in knitted dress and stilettos,
I note she still somehow manages, like Jackie Kennedy,
to wear grief with unintentional chic.

Old enough to know better
(Previously published in *A New Ulster*104; June, 2022)

We thought the real dividends from
those sisters' struggles would pay out once
we were unyoked from childrearing.
Admittedly, a little pang at the odd chum
whose youthful beauty, like a rose in winter,
blooms on, but no time for menopausal angst,

when in scarecrow couture, we show more concern
for havoc wreaked by weather on our plants
than on our faces. Become 'Fun Granny'
teaching grand kids to play poker and swear,
dye our hair a raffish blue
and do the rounds of summer festivals.

Then it seems the secret of eternal youth is out.
We must sand skin to a shine, pump up lips like lilos,
tattoo eye-brows drag queen arch…
And those of us adamant that, 'You won't catch me-',
still find our spirits sagging with our skin
at the thought of finding ourselves déclassé.

But sisters should be savvy enough to know
there is no fixing the clock on hands, neck, décolleté,
where gnarling, crumpling, creping,
contradicts their face's new youthful façade
and, always at odds, will be their eyes,
whose seasoned expression cannot be expunged.

Not as Young as they Feel

After gourmet sex,
they entwine like twins in a womb.
Doze under exhaustion's ether.
Twenty years ago even,
they would be free to slumber until morning.
But, in middle age,
sleep must be prepared for like a journey,
a check list of pills for pain, cholesterol,
blood pressure...
nightclothes, stripped off in present tearing lust,
are retrieved from floor, pulled back on,
sheets smoothed, pillows plumped, duvet adjusted,
the final pee. A 'Night Night' kiss
then, easing onto back and side,
the width of a double bed growing between them.

Card
(Previously published in *The Lake;* January, 2020)

I hesitate before buying the card;
unsure if it is still etiquette for baby-boomers.
A simple text might suffice now,
but somehow that seems more suited to
sexting, invites for coffee, 'I'm running late.'
Of course, her sisters may be instructed
to head off these well-meaning words
that do not, in fact, bring comfort,
but land on door mats like life's final demands
and will shove in drawers, until the grief
has down-graded from acute to chronic.

In Clintons, I scan banks of birthday, weddings,
Christmas cards. Finally find 'Bereavement'
tucked away like a pauper's grave.
Shake my head at brash designs,
with condolences bold as neon signs,
finally find one card, a hint of pastel flower with
'In Sympathy' whispered in lower case.

At home, the card lies on the table waiting
for the right words, until I sit with pen in hand,
mentally writing, then scratching out,
'Thinking of you, So sorry for your loss, Sad to hear.'

Instead a brief tribute to her husband.
Easy to talk to, edge-of-his-seat enthusiasm
for books, art, films…
and to her, an acknowledgement of our friendship,
going back some 50 years to the day we were shooed
away 'to play in the garden,'
whilst our mothers gossiped over
Darjeeling and Disque Bleu.
Later, I slow the car, mute the radio, whilst trying to
recall a red or yellow front door
to their fresh-start house,
thrust the card in, cursing the tell-tale letter box,
scurry back down the drive before I am caught
door stepping her grief.

About my mother's face

Mother was ordinary until classmates, staring at her
on Speech Day, squealed: 'Your mum's so pretty,'
her face becoming my own status symbol to rival
their parents' E-type Jags and mansions.

But as men gawped at her in the street,
a silent adolescent scream, 'Look at me too!'
Other times, catching my breath at her moss-agate
eyes that changed colour with her moods.

Paparazzi, snapping as she swept through Heathrow,
knew she should be model, actress or concubine.
Yet her ambition was to 'look out her kitchen window
and see a reliable husband digging in his garden.'

But no man could not imagine her stooping to vacuum,
so, she drew only prospectors and connoisseurs
who, licking their lips as if undressing Marilyn,
soon found they were fucking Doris Day, and left.

Proving to friends that 'Mother was a great beauty',
my present a solitary portrait, 6 by 5,
taken in middle age to celebrate her glamour's climax,
disfigured though by the expression of despair.

Single Bed

My 20s cribbed in chaste single bed,
I learnt like a liberated battery hen to
free range the double in my nan's spare room.

Discovered fecundity there,
not babies, but ideas that quickened,
books, paper, forming an academic counterpane.

Upgrading to my own double meant fancy linen
and fancy man for boudoir fun, then intimacy,
eyes meeting in the morning with a smile.

Our marital bed, a supersized super king
that ambushes visitors seeking the loo,
relegating my old double to the spare room

where to coppice space, amongst thicket
of wardrobes, drawers, you suggest 'chucking' it
for a single; my silence is miss-read as consent.

Your proposed downsizing has shades of the residential home;
Aunty Betty, her life contracted to a single bed,
whose only purpose now is a dreamless sleep.

connoisseurs of comedy

I remember his clowning,
all six foot of him,
spontaneously swung around
a lamppost, Tarzan hollering,
mum grinning but also scanning
the village high street like a fly pitcher's look-out,
in case his antics were witnessed by people
'they might know,'
whilst I, giddy with giggles,
'Do it again daddy'.

And when our neighbour set off in pinstripe suit
and briefcase to work in the city,
presumably in the ministry of silly walks,
judging by his extravagant goose step.
My father would mirror, just yards behind,
mum anxious to preserve her friendship with his wife,
stoppering her laughter to hiss
'You'll get caught Don'

I have no sound of his voice,
but his friends recall that he was

Peter Cook sharp, Tommy Cooper daft.
Apparently not a laugh out loud man himself,
so Monty Python, Marty Feldman, Dave Allen
were watched in silence,
his appreciation of a particularly good sketch
acknowledged with a smile,
whilst mum and I cackled throughout
until we got stiches, hiccups.

And whilst watching me wafting about
in a tutu was no substitute for shouting
on the touchlines at a son playing football,
it happens that as I grew up
comedians were always my rock-stars,
and endorphins my drug of choice.
Now I find a surreal riff puts me through my paces
far more than any crossword,
and gallows humour has certainly seen me through.
So, it's this connoisseurship of comedy
I think we might have shared,
pitching up to gigs at the Winter Gardens,
quoting the parrot sketch,
keeping our wits whetstone sharp for each other.

Staying put

At first whispered here say.
I think it's a tease, others dismiss with
'Never come to it'. Nevertheless,
the village collectively shudders.
And the farmer's application is nodded
through by mates on the council.
The field that cropped a healthy profit
from boot fairs, fun fairs, steam fairs,
has been bought by death,
who is setting up shop for a better return.

In April, a last visit to the circus
that has squeezed onto a
left over slice of land opposite.
Its jaunty tent painted in primary colours,
the laughter and cheers of kids
at Biffo the clown's antics will be at odds
with the black cars moving to the beat
of a silent funeral march,
the mourners dressed in grief.

I note, the prefab chapel already erected,
landscape gardens laid.
Two unmarked buildings fool no one,
here bodies will be dispatched in batches,
like a grotesque bakery.

And there is no concealing the industrial
chimney, that sickens, because I
have had too much truck with such places.
Later signposts appear on the dual carriage way,
a friend jokes 'not far to go then'.

For 60 years I have clung with ivy grip
onto this village. Where 4 ft grandmother
took no nonsense from horses tall as titans,
that she war worked on fields.
And father yearly rolled the dice at the soft fruit sale
on another crop of capricious cherries.
But afternoon adverts remind me
that as a demographic I have a
bull's eye on my back now,
scold me into thinking about
the practicalities of my own endgame.

Unexpectedly, comfort grows,
about not making the long drive
to burn up in some alien place,
rather retrace the rural lanes
that were my childhood's set,
to Boughton Crematorium,
where even death cannot
prize me from this village.

The Pleasures of Swearing

First time I discharge the F word,
a transgressive tingle like flashing my tits;
the guttural 'ck' satisfying as spitting.
Bloody, bollocks, bastard, milder
on my swearing Scoville scale,
but still lip-smacking, especially
when coupled with an obscenity.
Sometimes sophisticated lexis laced
with a jigger of scatological to create
a dirty martini malediction,
all served in a posh bird voice
that adds a keener edge.

Initially reserved for errant partners,
bullying colleagues, catty friends;
then traded as proxy punches with a couple
disputing disabled parking space in Windsor;
or hurled like grenades through the door
at smirking Italian girls in information booth
who mocked my accent.
But over time used promiscuously
for car drivers who carve me up,
flimsy bags that spew shopping…

Slippery slope to the C word then.
Whilst friends spell it out or mouth,
see-you-next-Tuesday euphemism;
I find its animal grunt gives relief from frustrations
at politicians, back stabbers, cancer...
Admit to only closet use though.

Need to guard against letting slip
these verbal farts at parties, family 'dos'
to startled faces of elderly relatives,
acquaintance' tuts,
then I must paint on a red face
with a girly giggled 'So Sorry.'
Aware, too, that their initial tang
can diminish like over chewed gum,
so occasional abstinence required,
where I only employ chaste lexis of a vicar,
until these pent-up profanities
strain at my tongue's leash again,
because once you have the taste for...

A Girl's Best Friend

Her 'Do you buy diamonds please?'
in Eastern European accent startles like a hold up.
I expect hard case in hoody,
instead get pretty young woman
with toddler and cumbrous pram.

A reverse ceremony, slipping off
white gold engagement and
wedding bands from her finger,
proffering in her palm,
'I wish to sell these please.'

Rings are popped on digital scales,
strict as diet weigh-ins.
Diamonds are quizzed
under Jeweller's monocle.
She jiggles the pram,
strains a smile at the child,

'£200'. The girl beams as if
a surprise scratch card win,
'A lot of money.'

The jeweller's hallmark cheeriness,
'Buy yourself something nice.'
She leaves to translate the twenties
into nappies, fish fingers, fuel-key top-up.

Debt and death lurk behind his
'We see it all', the manager countering
with 'the good stuff too',
weddings and birthdays.
But the glitter has been heisted
from the £500 pendant
I have ducked and dived to buy.

As I leave, the rings, their past
exorcised by cloth and polish,
are set in the shop's spangled window display.
Their second-hand status
rebranded for superstitious customers
as pre-loved.

It's my funeral-

It's all novelty funerals now,
as if having the last laugh on death.
But to me the punch line is still,
the cortege carries a corpse.

I'd prefer to be delivered direct
to the crem, just you following the
'private ambulance' in a mini shout out,
your leathers and motorbike the only black.

Later, a good dinner where chums
are dressed in bunting bright and
over brandy exchange anecdotes,
that have you all crying with laughter.